Contents

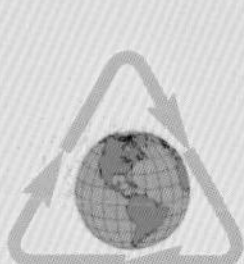
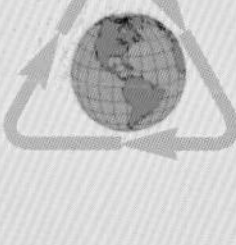

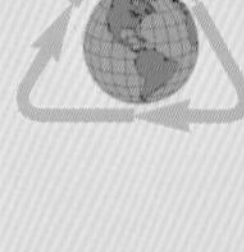

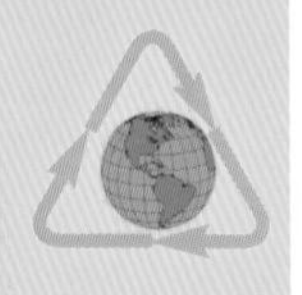

Is it really rubbish?

Some rubbish can be reused.
We can use, repair or make
it into something else.

An old chair (see page 15)

A pile of junk (see page 12)

Used paper (see page 10)

Making a Difference

REUSING Things

Sue Barraclough

W
FRANKLIN WATTS
LONDON • SYDNEY

First published in 2006 by
Franklin Watts
338 Euston Road
London NW1 3BH

Franklin Watts Australia
Hachette Children's Books
Level 17/207 Kent Street
Sydney NSW 2000

Original concept devised by
Sue Barraclough and Jemima Lumley.

Editor: Adrian Cole
Designer: Jemima Lumley
Art director: Jonathan Hair
Special photography: Mark Simmons (except where listed below)
Consultant: Helen Peake, Education Officer at
The Recycling Consortium, Bristol

Acknowledgements:
The author and publisher wish to thank Helen Peake and the staff at The Recycling Consortium. Green Glass (www.greenglass.co.uk); page 27. The Recycling Consortium; page 25tr. Images on pages 8, 9, 18b, 19br, 20, 23t, 26l supplied by the national Recycle Now campaign (for more information on recycling visit www.recyclenow.com). Topfoto Syracuse Newspapers/Image Works/Topfoto; page 21b.

Special thanks to Connie, James, Romi, Ruby and Tom for taking part.

A CIP catalogue record for this book is available
from the British Library.

ISBN-10 0 7496 6484 3
ISBN-13 978 0 7496 6484 8
Dewey Classification: 363.7282

Printed in China

Franklin Watts is a division of Hachette Children's Books.

Some old books and toys (see page 16)

Some old clothes (see page 18)

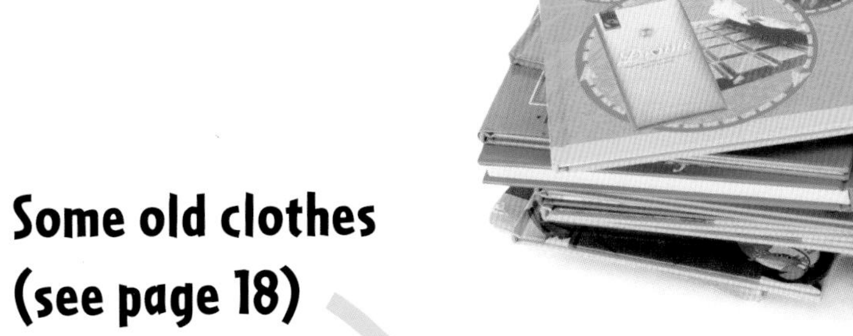

A damaged blow-up toy (see page 14)

If something has been used once, or is old or broken, do you throw it away? Try to find a way to reuse or repair it.

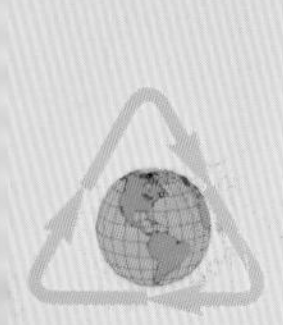

Why reuse?

Most of the rubbish we throw away is collected and buried in big holes called landfill sites. One day there will not be any more space to bury our rubbish.

When we reuse things, less rubbish is buried in landfill sites.

Reusing something makes the most of the time, money, materials and energy used to make it.

Reusing paper

One of the easiest ways to make the best use of paper is to use both sides. Use scrap paper for lists and doodles. There are lots of ways to reuse paper.

Make a paper plane

Used paper

Make a notepad or book
Print your own wrapping paper
Create a paper collage
What you can do
Make gift tags from old birthday or Christmas cards.

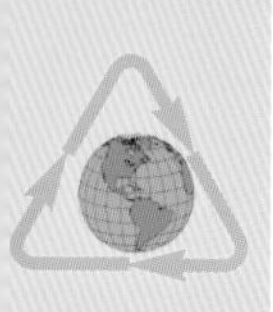

Reusing junk

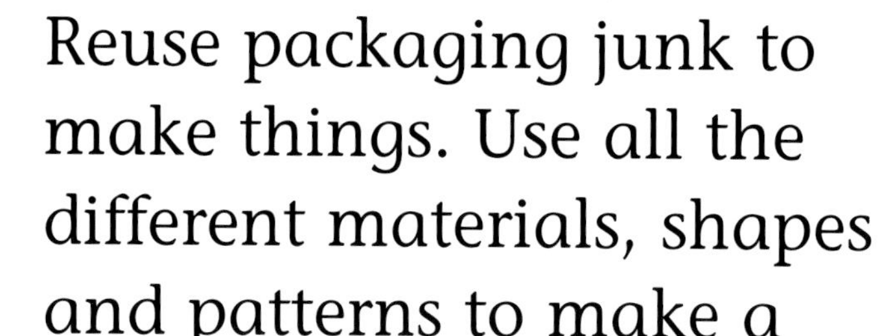

Reuse packaging junk to make things. Use all the different materials, shapes and patterns to make a monster model!

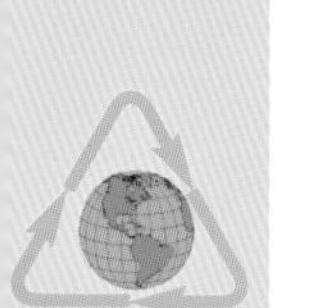

Look at all these ways of using something again.

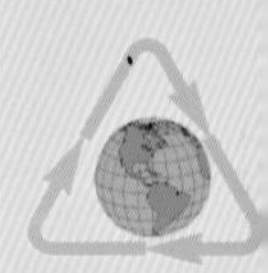

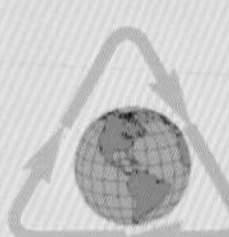

Jam jar pencil pot

Plastic bottle funnel

Egg box sorter

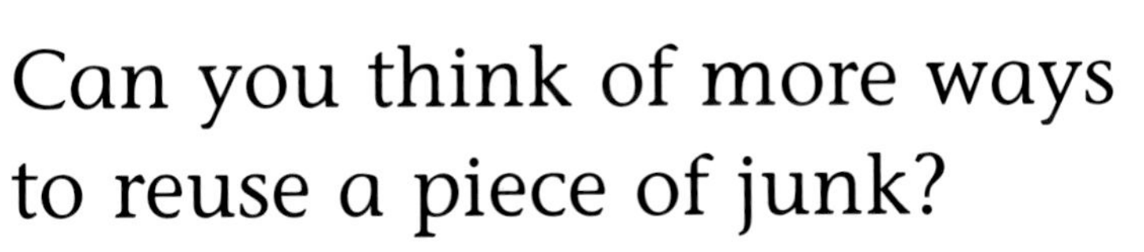

Can you think of more ways to reuse a piece of junk?

Repair and repaint

Sometimes toys, like this blow-up guitar, are easy to repair. Ask an adult to help you glue, sew or patch.

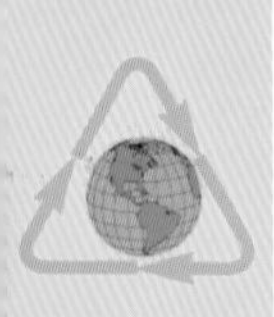

Other things, like this chair, can be repaired and repainted. Ask an adult to help you.

This chair was painted and decorated to make it look better.

Borrow and give away

Another way to reuse is to borrow books and toys from a library. Then you can take them back and get some different ones.

If you are bored with your toys or books, do not put them in the bin.

Pack them up and give them away to someone else, or take them to a charity shop.

What you can do

Give away books that you are too old for, or that you no longer read.

Old clothes?

Do not throw old clothes into the rubbish bin. There are lots of ways you can reuse them.

Post them into a clothes bank or take them to a charity shop

Renew clothes by adding patches and other decorations

Wear an old shirt as an overall for messy jobs

Did you know?

Millions of people across the world are too poor to buy the clothes and shoes they need.

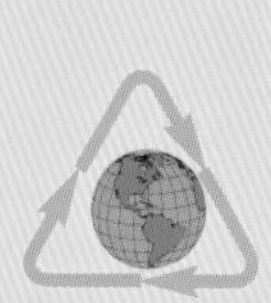

Buy second-hand

Another way to reuse is to buy second-hand clothes and toys. You can give the charity shop something you are bored with, and buy something that is new to you.

You can help to sort out your family's old clothes to take to a car boot sale.

What you can do

Look for garage or car boot sales in your neighbourhood. They are a great way to find new toys.

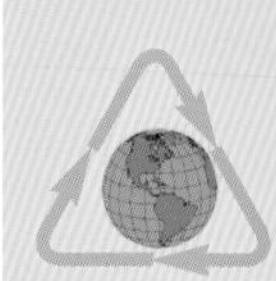

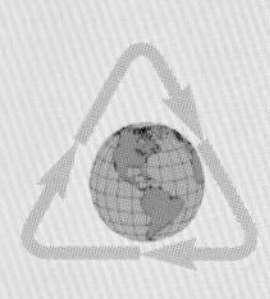

Reusing bags

Plastic bags are lightweight and strong. They are good for carrying shopping, but bad for our world. Plastic bags can easily blow away and pollute our country.

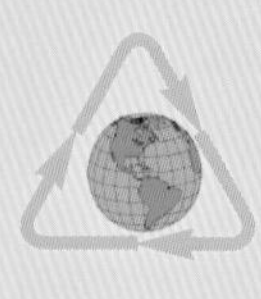

When you help to unpack the shopping, do not throw the bags away. Reuse them next time. Try using strong plastic bags that are made to be reused.

Cloth bags, cardboard boxes or a basket can also be reused to carry shopping.

What you can do

Make tiny bag bundles to put in your pocket. Then you will have a bag when you need one.

Choose to reuse

Many things are made to be thrown-away once you have used them. Think of disposable nappies, plastic cups, bottles and throw-away cameras.

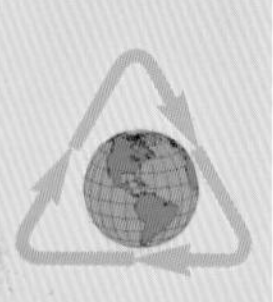

We should choose things that are made to last and can be reused.

Some nappies can be reused

A plastic lunchbox can be reused

Dangerous waste

Choose batteries that can be reused and help to reduce the dangerous waste sent to landfill sites. Only special batteries can be recharged.

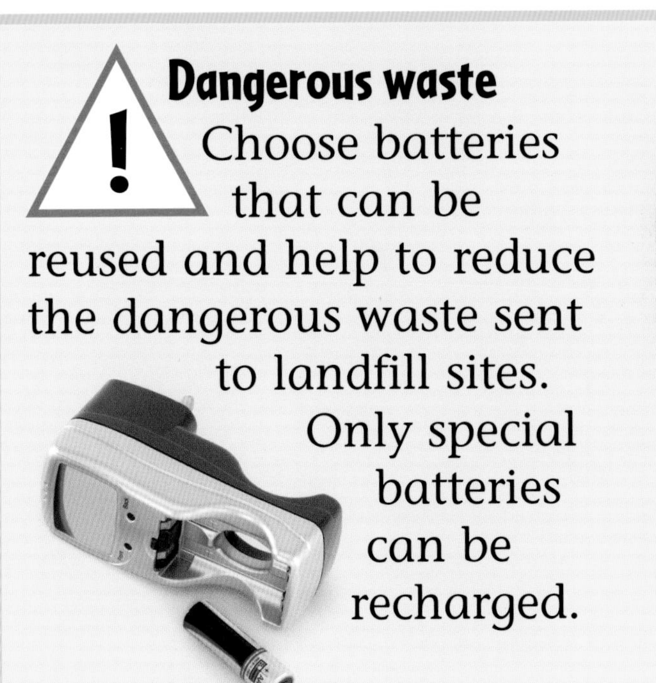

What's been reused?

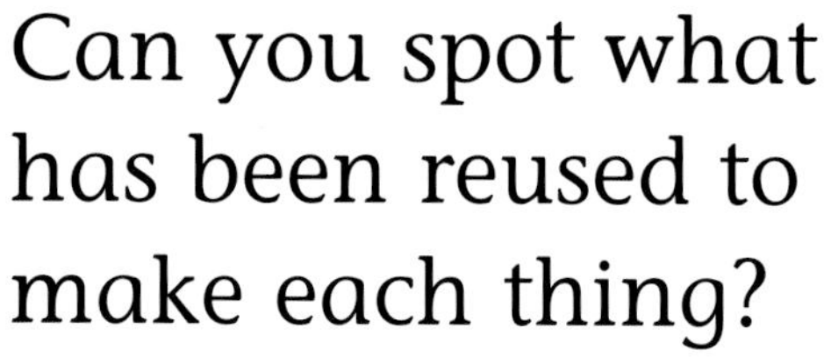

Can you spot what has been reused to make each thing?

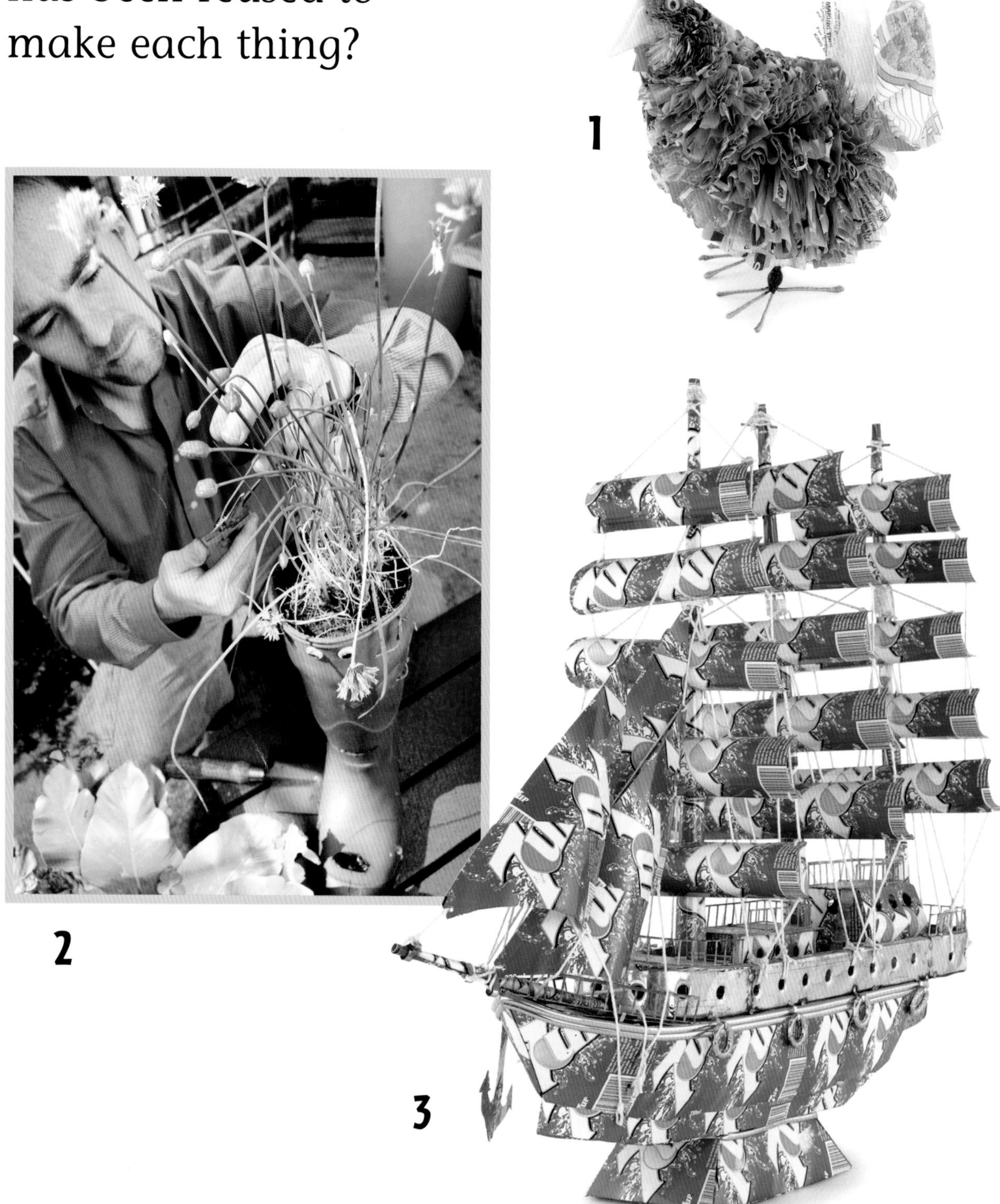

1

2

3

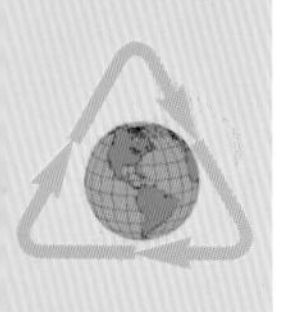

4

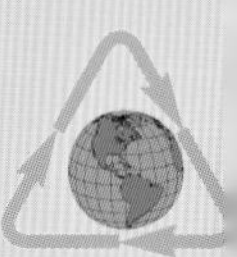

5

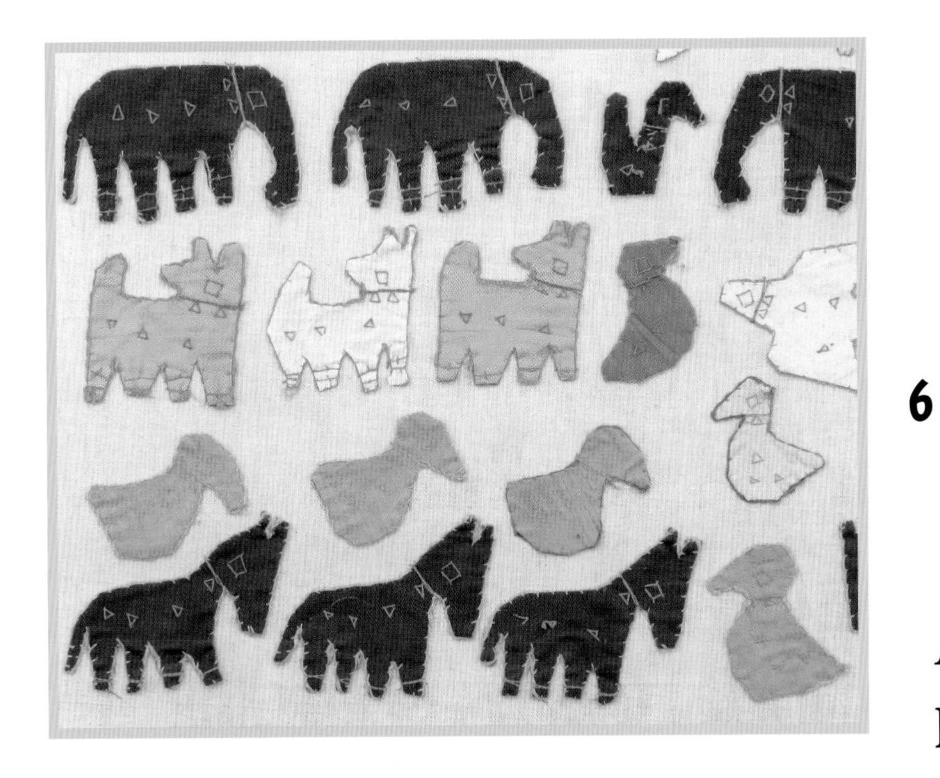

6

Answers on page 29.

Find out more

Reusing things means you will send less rubbish to landfill sites. Before you throw something into a rubbish bin, think of a way you can reuse it, or store it somewhere for when you need it. This way you will make the best use of the time, money, energy and materials used to make it.

www.make-stuff.com
A good website for ideas on reusing household items to make things.

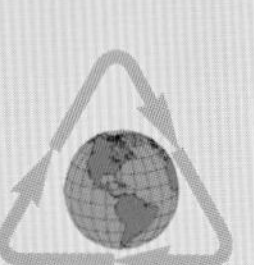

www.childrensscrapstore.co.uk
Find out where you can find reusable art and craft resources in your area.

www.planetark.com/campaignspage.cfm
Click on 'plastic bags – just say no' to find out more about this campaign in Australia.

http://scrap-sf.org/links.htm
Some great links from the Scroungers' Center for Reusable Art Parts!

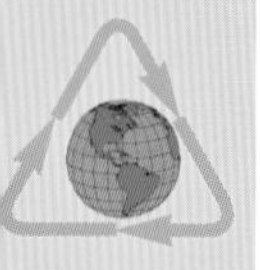

www.recyclenow.com
Type 'reusing' in the search box to discover lots of ideas on reusing and recycling.

www.reusablebags.com
All about reusable bags and other reusable items.

www.sort-it.net/how
Full of ideas on rethinking rubbish and reusing things.

Every effort has been made by the Publisher to ensure that these websites contain no inappropriate or offensive material. However, because of the nature of the Internet, it is impossible to guarantee that the contents of these sites will not be altered. We strongly advise that Internet access is supervised by a responsible adult.

Glossary

Charity shop – a shop that sells clothes, books or toys to make money for charity. A charity raises money for a good cause.

Disposable – something that is made to be thrown-away after it is used.

Landfill site – a huge hole in the ground that is filled with rubbish, then the rubbish is covered with soil.

Material – the substance something is made from. For example, paper is made from a material called wood.

Packaging – bottles, jars, cartons, boxes, bags, wrappings and containers. All these things can be made from different materials such as paper, glass and plastic.

Pollute – to make something dirty or poison it.

Answers to quiz on page 26–27: 1 – the chicken is made from plastic bags and other pieces of plastic; 2 – a wellington boot has been reused as a plant pot; 3 – drinks cans have been chopped up to make a ship; 4 – this drinking glass is made from a glass bottle; 5 – this bag is made from orange drink cartons; 6 – this animal picture is made from old pieces of fabric.

Index

About this book

Making a Difference: Reusing Things aims to encourage children to think about rubbish, to get the most out of different materials and to have fun by reusing them in a variety of ways.
Reusing things is a good way to reduce the amount of rubbish that is sent to be buried in landfill sites. Encourage children to think about the consequences of continuing to send huge amounts of rubbish to be buried every day.

Use **pages 10–11** to discuss how paper is made so that children can appreciate its value and why it is important not to waste it.
Pages 12–13 encourage children to think of ways of reusing household items.
Pages 14–21 look at a range of different ways to reuse things. Repairing and repainting helps children to value the time and energy used to make things.

Use **pages 22–23** to think about plastic bags and why the reusable alternatives are better.
Page 24 focuses on throw-away or disposable items. Discuss with children why it might be better to choose to reuse.
The quiz on **pages 26–27** encourages children to think about materials, to notice similarities and differences, and to see how they can be reused creatively.